GLIMPSES INTO SUTTON'S PAST

Part I
1800-1850

APS BOOKS
Stourbridge

APS Books,
4 Oakleigh Road, Stourbridge, West Midlands, DY8 2JX

APS Books is a subsidiary of the
APS Publications imprint
www.andrewsparke.com

Copyright ©2020 Stephen Roberts
All rights reserved.

Stephen Roberts has asserted his right to be identified as the author of this work in accordance with the Copyright Designs and Patents Act 1988
First published worldwide by APS Books in 2020

No part of this publication may be reproduced, stored in or introduced into a retrieval system, or transmitted, in any form, or by any means (electronic, mechanical, photocopying, recording or otherwise) without the written permission of the publisher except that brief selections may be quoted or copied without permission, provided that full credit is given.

A catalogue record for this book is available from the British Library

ISBN 9781789962123

IMAGES

Cover: View of Sutton Coldfield by Agnes Bracken. Reproduced by courtesy of Sutton Coldfield Library.
View of Sutton Coldfield by Agnes Bracken. Reproduced by courtesy of Sutton Coldfield Library.
View of Sutton Coldfield from Sutton Park by Agnes Bracken. . Reproduced by courtesy of Sutton Coldfield Library.
View of Sutton Park by Agnes Bracken. Reproduced by courtesy of Sutton Coldfield Library.
View of Sutton Coldfield by H.H. Horton. Reproduced by courtesy of Sutton Coldfield Library.
A Walk in Sutton Park by H.H. Horton. Reproduced by courtesy of Sutton Coldfield Library.
Four Oaks Hall by H.H. Horton. Reproduced by courtesy of Sutton Coldfield Library.
Hartopp's Pool by H.H. Horton. Reproduced by courtesy of Sutton Coldfield Library.
Perkins' Pool by H.H. Horton. Reproduced by courtesy of Sutton Coldfield Library.
Rowton Well, Sutton Park. Reproduced by courtesy of Sutton Coldfield Library.
Charles Barker, Headmaster of Bishop Vesey's Grammar School by John Griffin. Reproduced by courtesy of Kerry Osbourne.

For Matthew Williams & Sarah Brown

Acknowledgements

I would like to express my thanks to Kerry Osbourne for reading this text in its entirety and for his helpful observations. For answering queries of one sort or another, I am grateful to: Janet Jordan; Don O'Gorman; Len Smith; Stella Thebridge; Helen Thomson; and Zoe Toft. At Sutton Coldfield Library Abigail Collingwood has been, as ever, extremely helpful and efficient. All images, with one exception, are reproduced courtesy of Sutton Coldfield Library. That exception is the portrait of Charles Barker, reproduced courtesy of Kerry Osbourne. Thanks are also owed to Andrew Sparke of APS Publications for his work in ensuring this book saw the light of day.

CONTENTS

Introduction .1

I: The Warden & Society   9

II: Religion   15

III: Crime   22

IV: Schools   29

V: Leisure   36

INTRODUCTION

Between 1844 and 1846 three editions of a volume with the title of *Sutton Park and other poems* by Harry Howells Horton were brought out by the Birmingham bookseller and printer Thomas Ragg of Spiceal Street. Priced at 3s 6d, the volume could be found in many middle class homes in Sutton Coldfield. Horton recalled in his poem the joyous days he had spent since boyhood in the park. He would take his sketch pad with him, and drawings of such scenes as Hartopp's Pool, Perkins' Pool, Rowton's Well and Four Oaks Hall were included in the book. [1] Of the 104 pages of verse in the book, the poem about the park takes up 70 pages and is divided into two parts. It can be regarded as a superior version of the verses that tumbled off Victorian printing presses at this time - descriptive poetry that rhymed, with ruminations on such issues as poverty and drunkenness. Publication was funded by subscriptions, the conventional way of getting a poetry book out at this time: delighted that the poem was dedicated to him, Sir Edmund Cradock Hartopp of Four Oaks Hall took twelve copies. Horton's long paean to Sutton Park is a good place to begin this book: it presented the park and the town as tranquil, charming location, little changed over the decades:

> 'Sweet Sutton! Once again thy woods I view
> Which o'er my childhood a magic threw …
> While in the distance rising o'er the trees
> We view the old church tower – as if to please
> Still more the rapt enthusiast …
> And now sweet Sutton, let me turn once more
> To thy loved beauties, ere my task be over …
> T'was here my childhood's careless footsteps strayed
> Here my bright schemes of future bliss were laid …[2]

---

[1] Hartopp's Pool and Perkins' Pool are now known, respectively, as Bracebridge Pool and Blackroot Pool.
[2] H.H. Horton, *Sutton Park and other poems* (Birmingham, 1846), pp. 15, 41, 69.

Horton's depiction of Sutton was echoed in Agnes Bracken's *History of the Forest and Chase of Sutton Coldfield* (1860). 'Sutton may readily be spoiled – not easily improved', she wrote. 'Here, amidst her woods and heaths, the man, weary from the world's work, breathes freedom and refreshment.' [3] Richard Holbeche, a member of a prominent local family, remembered the town in the early 1850s unchanged for a century and the 'old field walks, old quiet lanes and picturesque black-and-white cottages.' [4]

View of Sutton Coldfield from Sutton Park by Agnes Bracken

In the first half of the nineteenth century Sutton Coldfield was an agricultural town. There were livestock markets and fairs, and auctions, often at the Three Tuns, of cattle, sheep, pigs, wheat, barley and timber. Many of those who lived in Sutton worked on the land; in 1851 farmland extended to 10,400 acres. The population grew steadily over this half century – from about 3,000 in 1800 to 4,280 in

---

[3] A. Bracken, *History of the Forest and Chase of Sutton Coldfield* (1860), p. 121.
[4] schlrg.org.uk/images/stories/transcriptions/My-Recollections-of-Sutton-Coldfield.pdf. p. 10. This handwritten diary has been most usefully transcribed by Janet Jordan.

1841 and 4,574 in 1851. The passing of a parliamentary bill in 1824 to promote enclosure in Sutton resulted in the transfer of 3,500 acres of common land into private ownership. The commissioner who oversaw the process in Sutton was John Harris, who held public meetings at the Three Tuns. [5]

Hartopp's Pool by H.H. Horton

The local elite were the great beneficiaries of enclosure. In his *History of Sutton Coldfield* (1891) the rector William Kirkpatrick Riland Bedford wrote about this development in entirely favourable terms: '… the material prosperity of the place was much augmented by this measure … it will easily be seen how much additional employment was created …' [6] Allotting the common land brought to an end the traditional rights of the poor of grazing stock and gathering fuel. In

---

[5] See, for example, *Aris' Birmingham Gazette,* 27 December 1824, 22 December 1828.

[6] W.K. Riland Bedford *History of Sutton Coldfield* (Birmingham, 1890), p. 47. For an excellent discussion of this matter see R. Lea, *The Story of Sutton Coldfield* (Stroud, 2003), p. 93-108.

the end enclosure was, according to E.P. Thompson, 'a plain enough case of class robbery, played according to fair rules of property and law laid down by a parliament of property-owners and lawyers.' [7]

Perkins' Pool by H.H. Horton

The most significant landowners in Sutton at this time were: Sir Edmund Craddock Hartopp and his son, also Sir Edmund Craddock Hartopp; F.B. Hacket; W.H.C. Floyer; Charles Chadwick; Joseph Webster; John Scott and the Revd. James Scott; and William Riland Bedford. The Hartopp family had purchased Four Oaks Hall – a seventeenth century mansion with an imposing columned frontage - in 1792, but were rooted in Leicestershire, with estates and a house at Knighton. In 1827 the deer park at Four Oaks Hall was extended by the acquisition of sixty-three acres of Sutton Park in an exchange of land with the corporation. This arrangement increased the size of Four Oaks Park to 109 acres, but was not implemented without strong

---

[7] E.P. Thompson, *The Making of the English Working Class* (1963), pp. 237-8.

opposition in the town.⁸ It was the custom of the Hartopps to provide a Christmas repast for their tenants in the grounds of Four Oaks Hall and, in September 1829, a hot air balloon, which had set off from Vauxhall Gardens in Birmingham, came down there after being in the air for over an hour. ⁹

View of Sutton Park by Agnes Bracken

Francis Beynon Hackett provided the land on which St. James' Chapel in Mere Green was built in 1835. His residence was Moor Hall, and he also owned Ashfurlong Hall, which he let. Joseph Webster was the proprietor of a burgeoning business manufacturing wire at Penns: he lived at Penns Hall and extended his estates in the area. ¹⁰ William Humberstone Cawley Floyer owned land in Walmley, but his main estates were in Staffordshire and he occupied Hints Hall. Related to

---

⁸ W.K. Riland Bedford *A History of Sutton Coldfield* p. 48 suggests this opposition extended to setting on fire the part of the park, known as Lady Wood, that Hartopp wished to acquire. In return 93 acres of land were presented to the corporation by Hartopp and a new main entrance to the park laid out.
⁹ *Birmingham Journal,* 3 October 1829; 5 January 1850. Four Oaks Hall became derelict after the Hartopps left and was demolished in 1898.
¹⁰ See S. Roberts *Webster and Horsfall & the Atlantic Cable* (Birmingham, 2020), pp. 8-10, 17-19.

Floyer, Charles Chadwick owned New Hall and its estates; after his death in 1829, the house was let and fell into disrepair, with the banqueting room being used as an apple store. The Scott brothers owned land in Maney, as did William Riland Bedford as part of a number of investments in the area.

Along the High Street lived the affluent middle class, in houses with gardens. These families needed professional men to help them in renting and buying and selling their houses and drafting their wills. Auctions of property often took place at the Three Tuns and from 1846 until his death in May 1860 Samuel Kempson, 'a cheery, bald man', was the auctioneer. [11] The solicitors were Edward Sadler and his son Richard Sadler and their competitors Thomas Holbeche and his son Vincent Holbeche [12] Serving these men and the shopkeepers, inn keepers, drapers, decorators, glaziers and other tradesmen of the town was the Sutton Coldfield Savings Bank, established in 1819, with Sir Charles Mordaunt and then Sir Francis Lawley, both MPs representing Warwickshire, as presidents. Within three years the bank had deposits worth £4,908 13 5d which had increased two years later to £10,532 11s 10d.

For more than four decades George Bodington was a notable figure in the town. He arrived in Sutton in 1836 and made his mark as a physician as well as playing a prominent part in the public affairs of the town. He purchased a private madhouse called Driffold Asylum, but also treated patients with tuberculosis, recommending to them exercise and exposure to fresh air. In *An Essay on the Treatment and Cure of Pulmonary Consumption,* published in May 1840 at three shillings, he 'advise(d) the patient not to neglect his ride or walk

---

[11] sclhrg.org.uk/images/stories/transcriptions/My-Recollections-of-Sutton-Coldfield.pdf p. 15

[12] Thomas Holbeche was based at 1/3 Coleshill Street from 1817. He and his son served as deputy stewards of the town. Another solicitor was William Steele Perkins in Mill Street; he was the son of the barrister Shirley Farmer Steele Perkins of Moat House. I am grateful to Kerry Osbourne for this information.

abroad, though the weather should be even severe.'[13] Licensed to the physician William Terry from about 1793, Driffold Asylum had nine male and four female patients in 1819 and eight male and six female in 1830 by which time it was being run by Richard Horton, also a physician. Under Boddington's new management, an advertisement for Driffold Ayslum offered 'a safe, cheerful and healthy retirement', with female patients provided with 'amusements and occupations suitable for them' by his wife Ann, and a complete absence of paupers.[14] Bodington became involved in the great debates about whether mechanical restraint should be used in asylums and his advocacy of such methods in the *Lancet* was to earn him a great deal of censure.[15] There were, of course, other physicians in Sutton, amongst them Thomas Chavasse, Robert Blick and Joseph Oates.

Though the corporation had, at a cost of £350, put cobblestones down in the centre of the town in 1792, all the roads leading into and through Sutton were subsequently maintained by a turnpike trust. This meant that travellers had to pay fees at toll houses to use the road. It was under these arrangements that, in 1824, the steep incline of Mill Street was reduced. It was reported that at this time stage coaches passed daily through the town 'for all parts of the kingdom'.[16] The drivers of these stage coaches became familiar figures to the people of Sutton, amongst them James Shore, the driver of the *Royal Dart* mail coach to Nottingham, who died at the Swan in May 1820. There were also omnibuses each day to Lichfield and Birmingham. To cater for the inhabitants of Birmingham who wanted to spend a Sunday afternoon in 'sweet Sutton' a Brookes omnibus left the town at 2.45 pm and

---

[13] *Birmingham Journal,* 6 June 1840. This review of Boddington's pamphlet is far from entirely approving.
[14] *Coventry Standard,* 2 June 1837.
[15] For Bodington's obit., see the *Lancet,* 11 March 1882. For a full account of Boddington's career see A. MacFarlane, 'Dr George Bodington 1799-1882: A Victorian Physician ahead of his Times' in *Proceedings of the Sutton Coldfield Local History Research Group,* vol. 11 (Summer, 2013). For the national picture see L. Smith *Private Madhouses in England, 1640-1815: Commercialised Care for the Insane* (2020).
[16] *Aris' Birmingham Gazette,* 19 September 1825.

returning at 7. 45 pm, at the cost of one shilling each way. The inhabitants of Sutton with money traversed the streets in post chaises or on horseback. The rest walked, inured to the stench but trying to dodge the manure.

Sutton at this time was a market town which proudly looked after its own affairs. There was considerable antipathy to surrendering decision-making to powers outside the town. This was evident in the feelings expressed at a meeting in December 1838 by those who paid the poor rate. With the passing of the Poor Law Amendment Act in 1834 Sutton became part of the Aston Union and the workhouse in Mill Street was closed and the inmates sent to the workhouse in Erdington. The meeting protested that 'the practical effect of the New Poor Law has been to prevent the parishioners from knowing the state of their own affairs.' [17] By the following spring there were plans to draw up for a petition to separate the parish from the Aston Union.

The existence of the workhouse reminds us that it was not just members of the gentry and the middle class who lived in Sutton in the first half of the nineteenth century. There was also a sizeable number people who were poor. It is difficult to get at their stories because of the absence of the records we have for other towns such as working class autobiographies. However, we do know that the Sutton poor were mostly farm labourers. They had regular work and kept pigs or grew vegetables if they could, but their wages were meagre, provisions were dear and their families were large. The agricultural poor of Sutton certainly knew hunger. [18]

---

[17] *Birmingham Journal,* 29 December 1838. See ibid., 13 February 1841 for a subscription which raised £60-70 to supply the poor with soup during the cold weather.

[18] See E. Griffin, *Breadwinner: An Intimate History of the Victorian Economy* (2020), pp. 197-200, 203-7. 209-10.

A Walk in Sutton Park by H.H. Horton

I: THE WARDEN AND SOCIETY

For the greater part of the nineteenth century Sutton Coldfield was governed, as it had been since 1529, by a corporation made up of a warden and society. This body of twenty five wealthy men was not elected but appointed by themselves and, when a member retired, another man of similar social standing was invited to join. It was, in the most literal terms, government by the elite. At the beginning of each November the members elected a warden. It could be better said that a new warden emerged for there were no contests. Richard Holbeche recalled that 'although everyone knew who was to be elected, it was quite proper to evince anxiety and later surprise.' [19] After a new warden was installed, the members of the corporation dined together. In November 1836, when the headmaster of the grammar school Charles Barker was elected warden, these gentlemen gathered at the town hall and 'most liberally supplied the table with venison, game, fruit etc.' [20]

The members of the corporation clearly enjoyed their dinners. In August 1825, a dinner was held at public expense when the Court of Chancery endorsed a plan that the income that the corporation derived from rents and the sale of timber felled in Sutton Park should be used for such charitable purposes as building schools and alms houses and the vaccination of the poor against smallpox. This expenditure was defended on the grounds that it was 'a trifling compensation to them for their gratuitous discharge of (their) ... duties ... besides it has been sanctioned by most ancient usage.' [21] Unsurprisingly the corporation was always at pains to make sure its support for the poor was reported in the newspapers – in May 1837 and in May 1842, respectively, four spinsters and four long-serving servants were given £20 each.

In 1800 the warden was Joseph Shutt and in 1850 it was Robert Garnett of Moor Hall. Over the half century covered by this book twenty-nine men served as warden, most of them for two years. They were not men without talent – Joseph Webster (warden, 1809-10) was an astute businessman, J.A. Oates (warden, 1845-6) was described as 'spirited' and Richard Williamson (warden, 1849) – a somewhat reluctant nominee - was rector and a former headmaster of Westminster School. [22] As magistrates, these men also dealt with minor offences, sending more serious matters to the Quarter Sessions and Assizes at Warwick.

---

[19] sclhrg.org.uk/images/stories/transcriptions/My-Recollections-of-Sutton-Coldfield.pdf., p. 22.
[20] *Warwick and Warwickshire Advertiser,* 12 November 1836. It was also a good day for local schoolchildren – they were given the day off.
[21] *Birmingham Journal,* 6 August 1825.
[22] Ibid., 24 October 1846.

With a small number of exceptions such as the Whig reformers Joseph Webster and his son Baron Dickinson Webster (warden, 1843-4) the members of the corporation were Tories, a sizeable number of them ultra-Tories. [23] This was reflected in an address composed in March 1829 in which the corporation declared the admission of Roman Catholics to the House of Commons to be 'dangerous'. [24] The repeal of the corn laws in 1846 was greeted with fury by the leading men of Sutton Coldfield. Members of the corporation – such as the physician George Bodington and the rector William Kirkpatrick Riland Bedford – were well represented in the Sutton Coldfield Association for the Protection of Agricultural and Native Industry, founded at the end of 1849 by Edward Swynfen Jervis of Little Aston Hall. Jervis' claims that free trade would lead to 'national ruin' and 'the downfall of the Empire' were highly persuasive to these men. [25] At a dinner for supporters at the Three Tuns in December 1850 Riland Bedford declared that 'as a body of men, the clergy, if not unanimously, were protectionists.' [26] This dinner proved to be the high point of Jervis' campaign; within a year his association had ceased to exist.

When a monarch ascended the throne or married or produced an heir, the corporation could always be relied upon to send a congratulatory address. To mark the coronation of Victoria in June 1838, it provided £50 to help pay for an open-air dinner for the poor. 'Three sheep, 800 lb of beef and 1000 quarts of ale were provided for the occasion', it was reported. [27] When Victoria got married in February 1840, the corporation paid for a cake and a glass of wine to be provided to 700 children; that evening they themselves attended a ball at the town hall.

---

[23] sclhrg.org.uk/research/transcriptions/2134-three-score-years-ago-by-helen-holbeche-1885.html p. 18 for a mention of 'a hot radical doctor' who used to decorate his house with reform flags during elections only to have them removed at night. This handwritten diary has been most usefully transcribed by Janet Jordan.
[24] *Aris' Birmingham Gazette,* 9 March 1829.
[25] Ibid., 4 February 1850.
[26] Ibid., 23 December 1850.
[27] Ibid., 2 July 1838.

Needless to say the warden and society had no intention of seeing themselves abolished. When the Municipal Corporations Bill sought, in 1835, to introduce elected town councils, the corporation drew up a petition to exclude Sutton from its scope and the warden William Edmund Craddock Hartopp made clear that he was in no mood to call a public meeting. This 'excited the just indignation of the inhabitants' and a meeting was held anyway and 500 signatures collected for a petition in favour of reform. [28] Despite this groundswell of support for a greater say for the inhabitants of the town in their own affairs, the corporation succeeded in getting Sutton removed from the bill. The corporation's desire to resist the reformers was bolstered by a speech at the annual dinner in October 1835 from Sir Eardley Wilmot, the Tory MP for North Warwickshire (which included Sutton Coldfield). Wilmot declared himself a reformer but stood firm against proposals which were 'not reform but revolution' and would lead to 'the government of this country ... (being) neither more nor less than a democracy' and 'subject to a Roman Catholic despot.' [29] One correspondent to a local newspaper observed that 'Sir Eardley is as fearful of applying new principles to old institutions as good housewives aforetime were of putting new wine into old bottles.' [30]

The warden and society met once a month and delegated detailed work to several committees. These men knew each other well, and mostly their meetings were extremely cordial. There was, however, 'rather an angry discussion' in September 1835 when a member of the corporation who had moved to Edgbaston cast a deciding vote in the appointment of the high steward, a largely symbolic post. [31] The Earl

---

[28] *Birmingham Journal,* 1 August 1835.
[29] *Aris' Birmingham Gazette,* 6 November 1835. Wilmot was MP for North Warwickshire from 1832 until 1843 when he was appointed lieutenant-governor of Van Diemen's Land. When he stepped down, he was presented with a gold snuff box by his supporters in Sutton. The 'Roman Catholic despot' he referred to in his speech was Daniel O'Connell, the architect of Catholic emancipation who was at this time working in alliance in the House of Commons with the Whig government.
[30] *Birmingham Journal,* 21 November 1835
[31] Ibid., 26 September 1835.

of Aylesford decided that one dubious vote was enough and accepted the appointment. He continued in the role until his death in 1859. Already unpopular amongst a section of the inhabitants because of his opposition to municipal reform, his appointment as high steward demonstrated the determination of the Tories to assert their control of the corporation.

The management of Sutton Park was a major concern for the corporation. Apart from the schoolmasters and mistresses, the two park keepers were the only people employed full-time by the corporation. They were each paid £50 a year and provided with a coat and hat and a house. The timber obtained from the park, of course, was an important source of revenue for the corporation. The park was attracting increasing numbers of visitors from outside the town, in the summer months amounting to hundreds a day. In an era when the rich harboured deep fears about disorder by the poor, there were alarming reports of the behaviour of parties of gypsies:

'The most disgraceful scenes of intemperance were constantly occurring and, at length, attaining such a height that respectable females could not walk in the park in the evening without danger of insult and molestation. Robberies have likewise been committed on several gentlemen who had endeavoured to restrain lawless individuals from the perpetration of offences.' [32]

The corporation was not slow to act. In April 1844 new regulations were made known, stating that parties from outside the town had to seek prior permission to enter the park, declaring their numbers, their location and the duration of their visit. If permission was granted, the applicant was provided with a card that could be checked by the park keepers. It seems likely that most applications were refused; but there were still episodes of fooling around to disturb the corporation. In August 1845 Baron Dickinson Webster, on behalf of the corporation, investigated reports of bathers in the park 'assembling in a disorderly manner.'; and in August 1849 a publican from Hockley Hill William

---

[32] Ibid., 29 April 1844.

Carter found himself before the warden and fined thirty shillings when he began selling beer to parties of gypsies he had arranged to visit the park. [33] A suggestion by a correspondent to a newspaper that the corporation should encourage the poor of Birmingham to visit the spring known as Rowton's Well was certainly not welcome:

' … I think it right, when there is so much talk about 'baths for the people', that the invigorating qualities of this delightful spring should be made known, particularly among the poor classes … I would respectfully suggest to the corporate body of the town of Sutton Coldfield that it would be as well to erect some convenience for bathers contiguous to the well … I shall perhaps to be told that, strictly speaking, the well is only for the benefit of the poor of the parish of Sutton and that therefore the corporation has no right to expend the parish funds in making it attractive to strangers. But let me ask if the poor of the parish derive all the advantages from the extensive destruction of trees that has been going on all the summer. The wood forms the principal feature of beauty in their park; and I should like to know what share the poor have in the profits realised by the sale of their timber …' [34]

Certainly the poet H.H. Horton enjoyed the colour and liveliness of a visit by gypsies:

> 'Assembled round the gypsy group is seen;
> And the wide feast is spread upon the green;
> The joyous song steals on the listening air
> While in chorus joins the happy fair;
> Then, hand in hand, the mazy dance they trace,
> Form the gay circle – part and then embrace;
> E'en infants seem to feel the merry joy,
> While ruddy faced old age sits jocund by.' [35]

---

[33] Sutton Coldfield Library, 'Minutes of the Warden & Society, 1832-1844', 11 August 1845.
[34] *Birmingham Journal,* 24 October 1846. The letter is signed 'A Rural Lounger', but I suspect it was H.H. Horton.
[35] Horton, *Sutton Park,* p. 39

An advocate of temperance, it was intoxication Horton believed that denied them their rightful access to Sutton Park:

> 'But see! Too oft they fill the social glass,
> And quaff the baleful draught – too soon alas!
> In ruder mirth and more uproarious joy,
> And loud dissentions they the time employ
> In reckless mood, the hanging boughs they break,
> As through the wood their maddening course they take;
> And hence the hand of power seeks to restrain,
> The few brief joys which to the poor remain.' [36]

II: RELIGION

In 1800 there were three places of worship in Sutton Coldfield. These were Holy Trinity Parish Church; Little Sutton General Baptist Chapel; and Hill Wesleyan Methodist Chapel. Within fifty years the number had increased to eleven. The additions were: Green Lanes Licensed School; The Coldfield Licensed Infant School; St. James' Chapel, Mere Green; St. John the Evangelist's Church, Walmley; Holy Trinity Roman Catholic Chapel; St. Nicholas Roman Catholic Chapel; Maney Independent Chapel; and Mere Green Wesleyan Methodist Chapel.

Holy Trinity was at the centre of religious activities in Sutton and the destination on Sunday mornings of the local elite. 'It was a sight to see them come into church, always when the psalms were being read', Holbeche recalled of the Hartopps of Four Oaks Hall. 'They would enter by the north entrance, walk into the chancel in single file, then down the middle of the nave and gain their gallery, while a flunkey, bolted by the side aisle, opened their door and escaped by a second into his own pew, as the party passed with ridiculous dignity. While

---

[36] Ibid. Horton was also the author of a lengthy poem called *The Pleasures of Temperance* (1843).

they were at the preliminary devotions, he popped out, shut down Sir William's seat and regained his place.' [37] Holy Trinity could accommodate 1,216 people, 420 of them in free seats; of the latter 300 were the property of the corporation for the use of school children. The average attendance on a Sunday morning was 600 (200 of them children) and on a Sunday afternoon 520 (170 of them children).

Four Oaks Hall by H.H. Horton

---

[37] sclhrg.org.uk/images/stories/transciptions/My-Recollections-of-Sutton-Coldfield.pdf, pp. 8-9.

The rector played a very prominent role in the affairs of the town. He was a member of the corporation and anything that was happening in public life he was involved in. He was a magistrate and a substantial landowner across Sutton. The incumbents during this period were John Riland (1790-1822), William Riland Bedford (1822-43) and Richard Williamson (1843-50). Riland was remembered for walking long distances across his parish, sporting 'his bushy wig, flapped hat and long cassock-like coat' and for that wig catching alight from the pulpit candles during a sermon. [38] He also did not keep a well-ordered churchyard. 'Pigs, horses and cows are to be kept out of the churchyard', he was told, 'and it is to be grazed only by sheep.' [39] Riland was, however, firm in his opposition to enclosure, declaring that 'I believe what the parish almost throughout believe, that it will prove a considerable and lasting injury to several hundreds of them.' [40] All of these men were Tories, but Riland Bedford was particularly active in party politics: in February 1833 he chaired a dinner to celebrate the return of the Tory candidates for North Warwickshire Eardley Wilmot and W.S. Dugdale in the general election a month earlier. Like many Anglican clergymen, Riland Bedford disliked the Poor Law Amendment Act of 1834, which brought an end to outdoor relief, and sought to persuade the Board of Guardians of the Aston Union to provide assistance without the poor having to enter the workhouse at Erdington. He collapsed and died after a confrontation in Birmingham in July 1843. He had driven his carriage into a pony and fell and struck his head during the ensuing argument; bleeding, a small amount of ammonia in water, ice applied to his head and mustard and hot water to his feet could not save him.

Richard Williamson was Riland Bedford's cousin. Educated at Westminster School and Trinity College, Cambridge, he was a man of a scholarly disposition. In 1825 he secured first class honours, in 1827

---

[38] W.K. Riland Bedford, *Three Hundred Years of a Family Living; Being a History of the Rilands of Sutton Coldfield* (1889) p. 131. Also see S. Ingelby 'The Riland and Riland Bedford Clergy' in S. Thebridge ed. *Holy Trinity*, pp. 205-8.
[39] Quoted in S. Thebridge ed., *Holy Trinity*, p. 148.
[40] W.K. Riland Bedford, *Three Hundred Years of a Family Living* p. 133.

he won a prize for Latin composition and in 1828 he became an M.A., a fellow of his college and headmaster of Westminster School. He spent the next eighteen years at Westminster, where he was remembered for taking a great interest in the production of plays. In 1835 he was awarded the honorary degree of doctor of divinity. Williamson knew that he would remain rector only until his predecessor's son William Kirkpatrick Riland Bedford was old enough to take on the role. It was an arrangement he was never at ease with. He entered into his new role 'with ... simple wishes and desires' which saw him take a great interest in the corporation schools - he served on the schools committee – assist in the formation of a subscription library, establish a women's club and recruit female members of the congregation to deliver tracts. [41] In his farewell speech Williamson made clear that his departure was 'an occurrence to which I have been looking forward and for which I have been preparing ... I have always looked on this parish as a temporary residence and not an abiding home.' [42] He moved on to become vicar of Pershore, on a lower stipend of £100 per annum. Williamson left Sutton with a silver tea and coffee service and remained at Pershore until his death in 1865. W.K. Riland Bedford later lavished great praise on Williamson: he was 'the best pastor who ever presided in Sutton ... his scholarship and high personal conscientiousness combined to cause him to excel'; it seems that Riland Bedford felt some self-reproach about the manner of Williamson's departure. [43]

The schools used for worship were owned by the corporation. The purpose of utilising schools was to ensure that the children who attended them could have no reason not to attend a religious service on a Sunday. Both schools provided could accommodate 100 people

---

[41] *Aris' Birmingham Gazette,* 19 August 1850. See S. Ingley, 'Sutton Coldfield Library' in S. Thebridge ed. *Holy Trinity,* pp. 118-19 for more detail about the subscription library.
[42] *Aris' Birmingham Gazette,* 19 August 1850.
[43] W.K. Riland Bedford, *Three Hundred Years of a Family Living* (1889), pp. 156-7. Also see S. Ingelby 'The Riland and Riland Bedford Clergy', in S. Thebridge ed. *Holy Trinity,* 211-12.

and the preacher was provided by the rector of Sutton. Green Lanes was licensed in July 1840 and provided one service on a Sunday afternoon, with an average attendance of 60 (30 of them school children). The Coldfield Infant School was licensed in September 1848 and provided one service on a Sunday morning, with an average attendance of 45 (25 of them school children).

St. James Chapel in Mere Green was also associated with a corporation school. It cost £1,500 to build, which was met by donations– including £100 from the executors of the will of Sir Robert Peel, who had died in 1830 - and a grant from the Incorporated Church Building Society. [44] On its completion, the workmen who built the church were provided with 'a good dinner.' [45] Consecrated in December 1835, the chapel could accommodate 582 people, 140 of the seats appropriated and 442 free. The average attendance on a Sunday morning was 289 (189 of them schoolchildren) and on a Sunday afternoon 297 (177 of them school children). The incumbent was provided with a house and by 1850 was in receipt of a salary of £150, only £22 of this being raised from pew rents and the remainder being provided by the rector of Sutton. Riland Bedford installed his former curate the Revd. Joseph Mendham as minister. Mendham was a prolific writer and editor, producing, amongst other publications, *Watson's Important Considerations; or a Vindication of Queen Elizabeth from the Charge of Unjust Severity towards her Roman Catholic Subjects* (1831) and *The Life and Pontificate of St. Pius V* (1832). He was able to read both Spanish and Italian. Holbeche described him as 'a tall, sad looking clergyman, a scholar and a book collector … his library was very valuable.' [46] Mendham was soon

---

[44] Sir Robert Peel (1750-1830) was the father of Sir Robert Peel, who was Prime Minister in 1834-5 and in 1841-6. He was a calico printer and built Drayton Manor, where he died. Founded in 1818 the Incorporated Church Building Society provided grants for building and restoring churches.
[45] *Aris' Birmingham Gazette*, 4 January 1836.
[46] sclhrg.org.uk/images/stories/transcriptions/My-Recollections-of-Sutton-Coldfield.pdf p. 17. W.K. Riland Bedford, *Three Hundred Years of a Family Living*, p.130 and S. Thebridge ed. *Holy Trinity* pp. 239 for Mendham and his library.

succeeded by Solomon Cadmon Saxton; he died in 1856 at the age of 88.

St. John the Evangelist's Church at Walmley cost £3,000 to build, all of it raised by subscriptions. Described as 'a remarkably elegant structure', it could accommodate 433 people and had an average attendance on a Sunday morning of 200. [47] The salary of the minister was raised from investments and rents from land, with both of which the church had been endowed, the rector of Sutton also undertaking to provide £55 annually. The pew rents were used to pay for a clerk, a beadle and for cleaning. The incumbent was the Revd. Gilbert William Robinson, described by Holbeche as 'a good but lengthy preacher.' [48] The Prime Minister Sir Robert Peel attended the consecration of the church in September 1845; the guests then retired to Penns Hall where they tucked into 'a most sumptuous cold collation.' [49]

Those inhabitants of Sutton with Catholic affiliations were catered for by two churches, where services were taken by two priests James Moore and his brother John or by monks from Erdington Abbey. [50] John Henry Newman also preached at both places. Holy Trinity Roman Catholic Chapel was erected in 1834 and could accommodate 250 people, 150 of them free. It attracted about 150 to the service on a Sunday morning and 50 to the service in the afternoon. In June 1850 the building – which was not insured - was damaged by fire, but the cause remained unclear. St. Nicholas Roman Catholic Chapel was erected in 1839 and could accommodate 50 people; average attendance for the Sunday evening service was about 40. The congregations at both these churches were made up primarily of Irish farm labourers. There was undoubtedly anti-Catholic feeling in Sutton. Mendham greeted the erection of Holy Trinity Chapel with a

---

[47] *Birmingham Journal*, 6 September 1845.
[48] schlhrg.org.uk/images/stories/transcriptions/My-Recollections-of-Sutton-Coldfield.pdf p. 8
[49] *Birmingham Journal*, 6 September 1845.
[50] I am grateful to Don O'Gorman for his help with this paragraph.

pamphlet entitled *An Address to the Inhabitants of Sutton Coldfield on the Introduction of Popery into that Parish* (1834). Its contents would undoubtedly have met with the approval of most Anglicans in the town.

The Nonconformist chapels in the town attracted only small congregations. The largest number attended Maney Independent Chapel, many of them travelling several miles. Erected in 1848, the chapel could accommodate 160 people, about 40 seats being paid for. The services were conducted by the Rev. J. Bourne of the Hurst Street Unitarian Chapel in Birmingham and average attendances were about 50 and 75, respectively, on Sunday mornings and evenings. The Little Sutton General Baptist Chapel had been erected in the middle of the previous century and could accommodate 60 people, with all seats being free. The average attendance for the morning and evening services was between 30 and 40. The chapel was supervised by the Rev. George Cheatle and his assistant William Snape of the Baptist Chapel in Lombardy Street in Birmingham, though services were often led by Edward Capewell, a packer and local preacher. The Hill Wesleyan Methodist Chapel and the Mere Green Wesleyan Methodist Chapel attracted sparse congregations of between seven and eighteen. The former was supervised by a steward John Stevenson of Hill Nook Mill.

It is difficult to calculate church attendance in Sutton at this time. The religious census of 1851 provides average attendances at morning, afternoon and evening services on a Sunday and, of course, some of these people may have attended more than one service.[51] Nevertheless we can be confident in saying that attendance was certainly above the national average.

III: CRIME

---

[51] K. Geary, *The 1851 Census of Religious Worship: Church, Chapel and Meeting Place in Mid-Nineteenth Century Warwickshire* (2014).

When it came to law and order, things carried on in Sutton much as they had in the previous century. Without an elected council as a result of its exclusion from the Municipal Corporations Act of 1835, there was no watch committee and the magistrates saw no need to make use of the Rural Police Act of 1839. Instead Sutton relied on a parish constable, sometimes supported by an assistant constable. At night a watchman, usually of advancing years, patrolled the streets. [52] Richard Holbeche remembers the parish constable as being 'a smart and soldier-like man.' [53] For many years the constable was Thomas Butler. He could be found in a house near the churchyard of Holy Trinity, and was known to almost everyone who lived in Sutton. It was his responsibility to attend crime scenes, question witnesses and make arrests. The constable had the power to call on the aid of local people: in November 1808 four young men were fined ten shillings each by the magistrates (which was given to the Sunday School associated with Holy Trinity) when they refused 'to assist the peace officers when called upon and for actively obstructing them in the execution of their duty.' [54] When a robbery or a burglary took place, the victim would send for the constable who was expected to arrive as soon as possible. The constable was not paid and learned about his role as he did it – which is why it was satisfactory to all concerned that Butler was willing to continue in the role for so long. He reported to the magistrates, who often took an active part in investigations. Minor offences such as drunkenness were dealt with by the magistrates themselves. When it was a more serious offence and needed to be tried by jury at the Quarter Sessions – which met four times a year – or by jury at the Assizes – which met twice a year - at Warwick, it was the constable who took charge of this. Devolving their removal to carriers did not meet with official approval because it

---

[52] sclhrg.org.uk/research/transcriptions/2134-three-score-years-ago-by-helen-holbeche-1885.html pp.8-9 for a description of one watchman, for whom the Holbeche family would put out a glass of beer and toast on cold nights.
[53] sclhrg.org.uk/images/stories/transcriptions/My-Recollections-of-Sutton-Coldfield.pdf p. 11
[54] *Oxford Journal*, 19 November 1808. A Sunday School for boys was established that year; one for girls had been in existence since 1806.

was discovered that the constable was claiming for more than he paid and the prisoners were 'often brought in a drunken and disorderly state by calling at so many road houses.' [55]

The moneyed inhabitants of Sutton Coldfield did not rely only on calling the constable if their property was entered. They sought to provide him with information that could lead to an arrest. This was achieved by setting up and funding by subscription a Society for the Prosecution of Felons. Such bodies existed in many rural areas. For many of these men an assault on their property was as serious as an offence could get. Almost all of the owners of property in Sutton subscribed to this association which offered a series of rewards if the person identified by the informer was convicted by the magistrates. For information relating to burglary, highway robbery, setting fire to ricks and the stealing or maiming of horses cows and sheep, the reward was £10; for stealing corn, pigs, poultry, tools, milking cows or receiving stolen goods, the reward was two guineas; and for stealing or destroying crops or breaking fences and gates, the reward was ten shillings. Often the victim of the crime added to these sums. If the informer had taken part in the enterprise, he or she was offered not only the reward but a free pardon if the name of another participant was provided. After about six years of existence, the association in Sutton disappeared in the early 1830s, suggesting that it wasn't as effective as its promotors hoped it would be. Nevertheless rewards continued to be offered for information leading to an a conviction in the most serious cases – when, in January 1839, a plantation of trees belonging to the corporation was set on fire, a reward of £50 and a free pardon for the informer (providing he had not started the fire) was offered.

Though highway robbery was in decline, it remained a hazard that travellers into Sutton in the early years of the nineteenth century had to contend with. In November 1802 a Mr Vernon, who was travelling from Birmingham to Sutton, was robbed of his purse containing £20 and a gold watch by two men on foot with pistols. It could have been

---

[55] *Warwick and Warwickshire Advertiser,* 1 July 1843.

much worse: it was not uncommon at this time to carry a great deal of money and Vernon had carefully concealed in a pocket book the enormous sum of £1,900 which the footpads did not discover. In June 1805 three robberies took place on the same day in the same place. In the afternoon a Mr Kendrick, who had almost arrived in the town from Walsall, encountered a highwayman 'who presented a pistol and robbed him of some gold and silver.' That evening the highwayman made two more appearances. He was described as 'a genteel looking man with fresh complexion, cropped hair and appeared about 23 years of age.' [56] He was not, however, apprehended.

Burglary was a far more common crime than highway robbery. In November 1800 the house of Thomas Hill was broken into in the early hours. Hill was tied to the grate and his wife to the bed and the intruders stole £50 and a quantity of cheese and bread. In September 1830 a Mr Barker woke up to discover that most of his wardrobe had been removed; a £10 reward was offered for information leading to a conviction of the men who had made off with Barker's coats, waistcoats, trousers, pantaloons, breeches, shirts and shoes. In November 1830 the house of Charles Cooper – who had served as warden in 1826-7 - was entered and a carpet, a hearth rug and a cheese were stolen. To the £10 reward offered by the Society for Prosecution of Felons, Cooper added another £2. There was great alarm in Sutton in autumn 1849 when a spate of burglaries 'of a most daring character' took place. Several houses a night were entered and 'thoroughly ransacked.' [57] Burglaries were not just nocturnal activities – in November 1850, whilst a Mrs Allcock was in church, skeleton keys enabled burglars to enter her house in Coleshill Street and relieve her of six sovereigns, her wedding ring and a quantity of silver. Burglary and robbery were regarded as more serious offences than assault. Thomas White, for example, was imprisoned for fourteen days for

---

[56] *Gloucester Journal,* 17 June 1805.
[57] *Birmingham Journal,* 3 November 1849.

assaulting Mary Hughes 'on the king's highway' whereas William Jones was transported for life for burglary. [58]

William Jones had entered the house of Ann Taylor in Wylde Green and made off with a quantity of plate, a musical box and about £400. A 75-year old widow with an income of £1,700 per year from rents paid in her native Liverpool, Taylor had recently arrived in the town. Jones had befriended two of the servants, making one pregnant and proposing marriage to the other. It was one of these two young woman who informed the constable that Jones had concealed the plate in a haystack. This was not the only misfortune that befell Taylor during the few years she lived in Sutton. She also found herself the victim of a charming, respectable gentleman who was also a fraudster. Francis Lloyd, a member of the banking family, had concocted a carefully-worked out plot to defraud Taylor. He was the magistrate who had investigated the earlier burglary and now ingratiated himself with regular visits and presents of fruit, game and flowers. Providing Taylor with a pass book and a cheque book, he began to make payments to himself. When he was unable to withdraw £1,000 from her account as requested and Taylor informed one of her rent collectors in Liverpool, Lloyd's scheming came into the open. Taylor began legal action to recover her money, and was awarded £1,281 in damages. This was the normal form of redress for such a situation at this time.

In an agricultural town like Sutton, a great deal of crime related to the theft of livestock and game. Stealing two ducks led to six months' imprisonment - as four unidentified youths discovered in January 1824. Stealing a single pheasant from the Hartopp estate led to six months with hard labour for James Smith and Sampson Benton in April 1830. Killing and butchering two of Hartopp's deer resulted in George Clarke and Matthew Stokes being transported for seven years in April 1844; they arrived in Van Diemen's Land, separately, at the end of the year. There was no escaping transportation when sheep or cows were taken: in September 1829 William Taylor and in July 1839

---

[58] *Birmingham Chronicle*, 25 October 1821.

James Needham learned that they were destined for new lives in Australia. The poet H.H. Horton condemned such punishments for poaching:

> 'He seeks the park, there sets the fatal snare,
> And lists the cries of the expiring hare;
> Crime leads to crime – at length, he spurns his home
> And reckless grown, he braves a darker doom ... [59]

Transportation was also the penalty for serious theft. When John Gerrard hired John Green and Moses Baker to convey him in a cart from Lichfield to Birmingham he foolishly showed off his bank notes; stopping at the Cup, they tried to rob him. Arrested by the constable, they were sentenced to transportation for fifteen years in January 1840. All of these men sentenced to transportation lived out the rest of their lives over ten thousand miles from Sutton Coldfield. To take just one example – John Green, who arrived in Van Diemen's Land in September 1842, survived until 1853, dying at the age of thirty six.

For stealing small but valuable items of personal property the sentence was imprisonment with hard labour such as the treadmill – three months for Joseph Moore in July 1822 for stealing a handkerchief, six months in April 1825 for Edward Evans for stealing a bed sheet, twelve months for John Robinson in April 1836 for stealing a hat, six months for David Grove in April 1837 for stealing a watch. There was a deep concern amongst the elite about juvenile delinquency – as thirteen year old Henry Morgan discovered in July 1841 when he was sentenced to one week in prison and a whipping for stealing a handkerchief. Women were also sentenced to imprisonment with hard labour. It was the fate that befell Mary Nevill and Elizabeth Nevill when they were sentenced, respectively, to six months and three months for stealing a pair of silk bracelets in August 1836. In October 1842 Elizabeth Peers received seven years for stealing a book. There

---

[59] H.H. Horton, *Sutton Park,* p. 22. Also see pp. 91-2 for another attack on transportation.

was a deep fear about theft by servants. Elizabeth Owen and Harriet Allbutt were servants in the house of Paul Moore and in July 1843 were charged with stealing a number of bottles of alcohol. Moore provided these two women with 'an excellent character reference … (and) recommended them for mercy.' [60] Allbutt was acquitted, but Owen still received three months with hard labour. At the Quarter Sessions cases were moved along with great speed. It was not uncommon for trials to last little more than fifteen minutes and for the jury to devote only a few minutes in the deliberation of each case; all verdicts were returned at the end of the day. The men who entered houses at night in Sutton usually belonged to organised gangs from outside the town and were rarely apprehended. Those who opportunistically stole handkerchiefs, hats and ducks were the poor and did so in the hope of selling them; instead many of them found themselves in the House of Correction at Warwick.

It was assaults on property rather than assaults on people that were sent to Warwick by the magistrates in Sutton. In the case of Mary Ashford, however, in May 1817 the warden Francis Hackett had no choice. This time assault had led to death. The case was to attract national attention as a picture emerged of 'a young girl … in the bloom and prime of life … of great personal beauty' and of her alleged assailant declaring that he had 'been intimate with her sister and I will have my connexion with her' and of the dramatic turn-of-events at the re-trial. [61] Mary Ashford was a servant who had left a dance at a public house in Erdington at about 11 pm on 26 May 1817 and whose body was found seven hours later in a water-filled ditch in Penns Lane. Abraham Thornton was a labourer, who after the two had spent the evening dancing together, had left the public house with her. Thornton was arrested and, at the inquest, it was decided that he should be sent for trial on a charge of wilful murder at the next Assizes. At the trial in August 1817 it was alleged that Thornton had raped Mary and thrown her into the pit, where she drowned. Whilst Thornton admitted

---

[60] *Warwick and Warwickshire Advertiser,* 1 July 1843.
[61] *Stamford Mercury,* 15 August 1817; *Lancaster Gazette,* 22 November 1817

to having had sexual intercourse with Mary, his witnesses provided him with an alibi and he was acquitted of murder and rape. The verdict 'excited universal astonishment.' [62] It was claimed that 'the alibi was founded on the most uncertain evidence possible to advance – the opinion of country persons as to the time derived from country clocks.' [63] With this groundswell of public opinion behind him, Mary's elder brother William Ashford decided on an appeal. All those present at the appeal at Westminster Hall in November 1817 were astonished when Thornton challenged Ashford to trial by combat. In the event this did not happen, and in April 1818 Thornton was discharged. He subsequently emigrated to America. Mary Ashford was buried at Holy Trinity.

In Sutton and elsewhere it was widely believed that a guilty man had escaped the punishment he deserved. Over a quarter of a century later he was 'vehemently denounced' by H.H. Horton in *Sutton Park:*

'In the gay circle of the dance he met,
The maid on whom his lustful eye was set;
He drew his victim from the festal throng,
And o'er the Coldfield wandered long.
In vain he tried to lure her guileless heart,
From Virtue's long-loved precepts to depart;
Abashed, the maiden from the monster flew,
Fired by revenge, the murderer's steps pursue,
Till faint with fright the struggling beauty falls,
And on the wretch for mercy vainly calls.
With coward heart he dreads the dawning day,
And to rush-grown pond he drags his prey;
No hand was there the innocent to save,
The winds moaned piteous o'er her watery grave;
And since then 'tis said the weeds have ceased to grow,
And the sweet wild-flower on the spot to blow ...'

---

[62] *Sun (London),* 11 October 1817.
[63] *York Herald,* 22 September 1817.

In a footnote Horton made clear that he was not prepared to modify his lines: '… even supposing that he was guiltless of the crime of actual murder and (putting it in the mildest light) that he was only the seducer, and that self-destruction was the result, we are still warranted in holding him morally responsible for her blood – and I feel justified in affixing to his name the indelible brand of MURDERER.' [64] It was an opinion most likely shared across Sutton. In July 1848 another case of assault caused outrage in the town. As she walked home from Sunday School, an eight year old girl was enticed into an empty house by Jabez Day, given a shilling and raped. This time justice was seen to be done: Day was transported for fifteen years.

IV: SCHOOLS

For the children of the agricultural labourers, spade-makers and blacksmiths of Sutton there were, in the first quarter of the nineteenth century, only limited opportunities to learn to read and write. There were dame schools in the area - where a widow or spinster took in a small number of younger children – but we don't know how many or whether they taught much more than the alphabet. [65] There were also Sunday Schools, established for girls and boys in, respectively, 1806 and 1808. Here the bible was read aloud and the children were taught basic literacy skills by members of the congregation of Holy Trinity. Admission was strictly controlled and those who behaved were rewarded with clothing and those who misbehaved found their parents complaining about fines. There were no schools in Sutton run by the National Society for Promoting the Education of the Poor, a Church of England body founded in 1811.

---

[64] H.H. Horton, *Sutton Park*, p. 59; N. Clifford, *The Murder of Mary Ashford: The Crime that Changed English Legal History* (2018) for the full story.
[65] sclhrg.org.uk/research/transcriptions/2134-three-score-years-ago-by-helen-holbeche-1885.html pp. 3-5 for a description of a dame school run by a Mrs Birch, who was took girls aged two and three and was effectively a child minder.

The decision by the Court of Chancery in 1825 that the income of the corporation from the felling of trees in the park should be used for charitable purposes transformed the situation. Within a year four schools were in operation. The corporation school in the centre of the town accommodated 100 boys and girls; the girls were taught not only reading, writing and arithmetic but also, in what was called a 'school of industry', sewing, spinning and knitting, producing clothes for both themselves and the boys and also blankets for poor married women about to give birth. The schools at Hill and at Little Sutton also accommodated 100 pupils whilst that at Walmley was smaller, with a class of 40. Pupils were admitted to these schools at the age of six and remained there until the age of twelve.

The schools operated according to the principles of the National Society. They followed the curriculum in national schools and the schoolmasters were assisted by pupil-teachers. The schoolmistress at the school in the centre of the town was assisted by another female to help the girls make clothes. She paid for this assistant from her annual salary of £60. The schoolmasters were paid an annual salary of £40 (£25 at Walmley) and provided with a house (into which they were permitted to take boarders), and the schoolmistress at Hill was paid £30. [66] The masters of the school in the centre of the town did not remain long: we can identify in the 1830s Mr Watton and Mr Phillips and in the 1840s George Meaby, William Felton and Matthew Wilson. [67] At first the salaries that were paid also covered the cost of coal, but in 1828 an allowance of £30 was introduced. There was firm control in these schools: absence of one day resulted in a fine of one penny and, if absences reached fifty days, pupils were denied free clothing. There were, however, also occasional treats. In summer 1848, having listened to 'a most interesting address' from the rector, the children of

---

[66] *Birmingham Journal,* 2 March 1850 for an advertisement for the post of schoolmistress at Hill. By then the annual salary had increased to £35, with an additional £5.10s for coal, and a house with a garden was provided. Also see A. Bracken, *History of the Forest and Chase of Sutton Coldfield,* p. 131

[67] See *Aris' Birmingham Gazette,* 7 March 1837; 20 October 1839; 11 June 1841, 12 January 1846.

the Sunday Schools were provided with 'an excellent dinner' before joining the pupils of the corporation schools for games and tea and cake in Sutton Park [68] In 1838 the corporation erected, with support from the headmaster of Bishop Vesey's Grammar School, a school to cater for 24 middle class boys in Church Hill, with fees ranging from 2s 6d to 10s. [69] By 1850 the corporation was operating seven schools, catering for 600 pupils. These pupils were expected to attend church on Sundays; at Holy Trinity the galleries were extended to accommodate them separately from the congregation. The objective in providing these corporation schools was to ensure compliance: the children were regularly reminded of what was expected of them in terms of behaviour and hard work and often found themselves singing the National Anthem. 'These ... (schools) are found fully sufficient for the wants of all the lower classes', a member of the corporation declared. [70]

There were a number of private schools across Sutton in which married middle class women and their daughters, and sometimes just the daughters, took in a small number of girls as boarders. We know of schools run by a Mrs Barr and her daughters and by Misses A. and M. Davis in the mid-1820s. During the 1830s and 1840s a school was run by the Misses Clues, and, at Maney House, Miss Birch also opened her own school. At these establishments girls learned the correct use of grammar, how to converse in French, singing and how to play a musical instrument. Some families advertised for tutors for their daughters– for example, in 1824 there was an advertisement for a young lady 'competent to instruct in English grammar, geography and the use of globes.' [71] There were also a number of private schools offering instruction for young boys – including one run by Lucy Riland of the clerical family.

---

[68] *Birmingham Journal,* 17 June 1848.
[69] This school closed in 1853.
[70] *Aris' Birmingham Gazette,* 4 May 1840.
[71] Ibid., 29 March 1824.

In 1800 Sutton Coldfield Grammar School – known to the inhabitants of Sutton as Bishop Vesey's Grammar School – was approaching its 300th year of existence. The affairs of the school, including its extensive ownership of land, were nominally overseen by trustees, of about 20 in number. The trustees were drawn from the leading families of the area – the Adderleys of Hams Hall, the Dilkes of Maxstoke Castle, the Floyers of Hints Hall and so on – and, in due course, the clergy. Meetings of the trustees were not always regular, and often only a small number attended. They might, for example, give the headmaster permission to sell timber from the school's estates to fund improvements. Their most important task was the appointment of a headmaster, to whom a great deal of authority was devolved. When the post needed to be filled, the net was widely cast, with advertisements placed in regional newspapers across the country. These men were expected to be graduates of one of the universities and members of the Church of England. Their salaries came from the rents paid by the tenants on land owned by the school; these provided William Webb, headmaster between 1768 and 1817, for example, with an annual income for all expenses, including an assistant master, of £200. The headmasters of the grammar school also considered themselves scholars and literary men. Charles Barker, who was headmaster between 1817 and 1842, wrote verse. These lines find him reflecting on the charms of Sutton Park:

> 'Before us winds the rural way,
> Across yon stream with alders gay;
> Up yonder gorse-crowned hill …
> 'In Nuthurst's windings would you stray,
> Or o'er wild heath & length'ning way,
> That leads to Rowton's Well?
> Pellucid fount! What annual scores
> Thy stream to cleanliness restores … [72]

---

[72] Quoted in K. Osbourne, *A History of Bishop Vesey's Grammar School: The First 375 Years* (1990), p. 80. For a full account of the grammar school during these years see ibid., pp. 46-125.

Charles Barker Headmaster of Bishop Vesey's Grammar School

James Eccleston, who held the post from 1843 until 1849, was the author of *A Conversation between an English Clergyman, a Romish Priest and an Independent Minister* (1845), which cost one shilling, with the profits of being donated to the newly-established church at Walmley; and *An Introduction to English Antiquities* (1847), an immensely detailed political, social and economic history of England up to 1689 which he dedicated to the governors of the school. The headmasters of the grammar school moved in the upper echelons of Sutton society, and played a leading part in local affairs. Barker counted the rector William Riland Bedford and the wire manufacturer Joseph Webster at Penns Hall as close friends. In 1772, 1836-7 and 1848 Webb, Barker and Eccleston were, respectively, elected warden.

The school catered for 'young gentlemen.' [73] The sons of such leading figures in the town as Thomas Holbeche, J.P. Oates, George Bodington and Samuel Kempson were all educated there. The 'young gentlemen' studied Latin, Greek and English without payment, and arithmetic, for which there was a weekly fee. It seems clear that for Barker the standing of the school was never his most important concern. He paid particular attention to the income the estates generated, happily agreed to becoming warden, frequently went out fox hunting and spent as much time as he could in the company of the Sutton elite. [74] Whilst he was doing these things, an assistant master was taking the classes in Latin. Unfortunately Barker had chosen a weak master, as one father observed in a remarkable letter about his son's progress: 'I must say I feel great dissatisfaction that he is not instructed by a person who knows something of the language he is learning. It is a mystery to me to know how a person can teach that which he is himself totally ignorant ... I am informed that there are boys who have been at Latin Grammar for two years and know nothing of it yet.' [75] It was not to be the last complaint, but Barker was unperturbed. He even went as far as converting the school room into a dining room for himself. He was in fact intent on reducing what he had to do. To this end he embarked on a plan of narrowing the curriculum to just Latin and Greek – a move which explained his desire to see a middle class school established in Sutton to teach other subjects. During most of his tenure only between three and six boys were attending the school; by 1840 this had become one, the son of William Felton, a schoolmaster at the corporation school in the centre of the town. In Sutton there was great disgruntlement at these unhappy developments. [76] When Barker died after falling from his horse as he

---

[73] *Aris' Birmingham Gazette,* 11 May 1835.
[74] See S. Trowbridge, *Holy Trinity,* p. 77 for Barker's novel arrangements for the pews reserved for the pupils of the school.
[75] Quoted in K. Osbourne, *A History of Bishop Vesey's Grammar School,* p. 57.
[76] See *Aris' Birmingham Gazette,* 4 May 1840 for a report of a meeting in which it was felt that 'the benefits arising from such a school are very limited.'

returned from a visit to his friend Joseph Webster at Penns Hall in October 1842, it was clear that a turning point had been reached.[77]

After a great deal of local controversy over fees, new arrangements were introduced into the grammar school in 1844. [78] The trustees became governors and the curriculum now embraced not only Latin and Greek, but also reading and writing, mathematics, geography, history. [79] For these new subjects, there was a fee. There was also a new headmaster, selected from 70 applications – James Eccleston, who had distinguished himself at Trinity College, Dublin. Eccleston received an annual salary of £300 whilst a new assistant master secured an annual salary of £100 plus one quarter of the fees paid. The reports of the men who conducted the annual examinations of the pupils at the beginning of each year were encouraging: in 1845 their work was described as 'highly commendable' and in 1848, as far as Latin was concerned, 'several boys reading for different universities are mentioned in high terms of praise.' [80] In an effort to increase recruitment, Eccleston declared that the school 'presents peculiar advantages, especially to youths from the colonies.' [81] Within a few years the number of boys had increased to 27 – though none of them came from outside the area, let alone from outside the country. Unfortunately Eccleston's appointment did not turn out to be the new start that was hoped for 'this dormant seminary.' [82] The headmaster ran up considerable personal debts, and, in May 1849, resigned. Shortly afterwards he emigrated to Australia with his family; in under a year he was dead.

---

[77] See ibid., 24 October 1842. At the inquest the jury returned a verdict of 'dying by visitation of God.'
[78] See ibid., 4 September 1843. The Birmingham solicitor Thomas Slaney who represented those who objected to paying fees observed that 'scarcely a dozen persons in the whole parish can be found who approve of the scheme ...'
[79] See ibid., 13 May 1844.
[80] Ibid., 6 January 1845, 3 January 1848.
[81] Ibid., 15 July 1844.
[82] See ibid., 9 November 1843.

VI: LEISURE

During these years the rural outskirts of Sutton became the location for a number of prize fights. These encounters, in which two bare-knuckled fighters often slogged it out over many rounds, could attract very large crowds, many of the Fancy, as the supporters of the sport were called, travelling long distances to be present. For devotees the attraction of the fights was seeing how much punishment the men could take and if they had laid their bets on the winning man. [83] The crowds extended across the classes – from those who had arrived in carriages and those who had walked. A prize fight that took place on the outskirts of Sutton in October 1816 was reported in newspapers across the country. A contemporary estimate claimed that as many as 10,000 people watched Griffiths of Sutton and Bayliss of Wednesbury confront each other for four hours over a staggering 215 rounds. Griffiths was the favourite, knocking Bayliss down in each of the first eight rounds and drawing blood in the second. But Bayliss held out against this onslaught. 'The blows, even to the last rounds, were given with the most tremendous force', a newspaper correspondent wrote, 'fully evincing the bottom of the combatants and their determined spirit.' [84] With both men exhausted, it was agreed that they should share the purse of £40.

The magistrates often sought to break up prize fights, but did not do so when Griffiths took on Bayliss. Given the large numbers arriving to witness the spectacle in the days before, it is difficult to believe that they were unaware of the fight and it seems plausible that the presence of many gentlemen in the crowd was the reason their inaction. However, when a smaller event in front of a crowd made up of working men took place in October 1827, the fighters John Clarke and James Hyde, both of Aston, were brought before the magistrates. The matter was settled when they undertook not to offend again, paid the expenses of the hearing and donated £1 to the national school at

---

[83] For a full discussion of pugilism see B. Wilson, *Decency and Disorder* (2008), pp. 288-95.
[84] *Liverpool Mercury,* 25 October 1816.

Erdington. This was not to be the last attempt to stage a prize fight on the outskirts of Sutton. A contest took place between George Dukes and Joseph Devy in April 1835, and it ended in the death of Devy. 'The combatants had fought for twelve rounds and the deceased appeared to be the winning man and had knocked his opponent down in the twelfth round', it was stated. 'Whilst he was sitting on Chambers' knee, the deceased smiled at Dukes and then threw back his head and died directly.' The Sutton magistrates sent Dukes to the Assizes at Warwick where he faced a charge of manslaughter. The jury found him not guilty after deliberating for twenty minutes. 'Dukes, you have had a narrow escape', the judge remarked, 'a narrow escape.' [85]

Angling, shooting and coursing all took place in Sutton Park. A licence from the corporation was required to fish in the pools; in the 1820s the landlord of the Cup Thomas Brentnall imaginatively arranged a subscription list to share the cost of fishing in Wyndley Pool. The park was not, however, highly regarded as a place to shoot birds. There were complaints at the paucity of birds and it was claimed that the park 'is nominally, but not effectively, preserved by the corporation of Sutton Coldfield or the game would be far more abundant than it is.'[86] Horton made clear his dismay at seeing hare coursing in the park and the presence of females amongst the spectators:

> 'Save when, on yonder hill, the crowds resort,
> Lured by the name of fashion and of sport.
> Then do the echoes of these woods reply
> To shouts of barbarous and impetuous joy.
> There, too, the angel sex by fashion drawn,
> Refuse on cruel sports to pour their scorn;
> That sex whose virtues are the theme of song,
> Cheer with their smiles the rude insensate throng,
> And, like th' Athenian fair, with eager eyes,

---

[85] *Aris' Birmingham Gazette,* 10 August 1835.
[86] Ibid., 6 December 1845

Pursue the rapid courser as he flies.
Oh, that this park, so long the rustic's pride,
Should be at last to senseless sports applied.'[87]

In 1844 a race course was constructed at Holly Knoll in Sutton Park. [88] It was oval in shape, about a mile in length and almost entirely fenced. A temporary grandstand was constructed; the permanent grandstand that followed was completely destroyed by fire in April 1846. Clearly a financial arrangement had been reached with the corporation, but there were 'many obstacles and annoyances … thrown in the way by a few of the inhabitants of Sutton.' [89] The considerable cost of the enterprise was met by a committee of Sutton and Birmingham men, of whom the most active were John Wiggan and T.S. Wilkins. Races took place on two days each June, and subscriptions were raised to meet the costs of each event. The races attracted large crowds of spectators from Birmingham and a large detachment of police from that town were brought in to keep order. In 1850 'many indecencies' led to the prohibition of bathing in nearby Blackroot Pool. [90] From summer 1844 races such as 'The Sutton Park Stakes', 'The Wyndley Pool Stakes' (the winner of which secured a silver mounted whip), 'The Cup Handicap' (the winner of which secured a silver cup) and the 'Hurdle Race' with 'gentleman riders' were being run. [91] There was a betting arena and booths where publicans from Birmingham sold ale, spirits and food. Subscriptions, however, were not always easy to raise. In March 1852 the corporation refused permission for a steeple chase across the park and that summer the race course held its final races.

The gentlemen of Sutton founded a cricket club in August 1847. The meeting at the town hall was 'respectably but not numerously

---

[87] Horton, *Sutton Park*, p.21
[88] See M. Holder, *The Archaeology of Sutton Park* (2013), pp. 145-7.
[89] *Birmingham Journal,* 14 July 1849.
[90] Ibid., 22 June 1850.
[91] Ibid., 17 June 1844.

attended' and the solicitor Henry Addenbrooke, the Revd. Richard Williamson and the schoolmaster Matthew Wilson became, respectively, secretary, treasurer and curator. [92] The Sutton men readily found other clubs in the area to compete with – Oscott College, West Bromwich, Lichfield and Burton. Sutton, like other clubs, brought in a professional cricketer to help with training. The season lasted from June until October. In September 1849 there was a match with a combined team from Burton and Lichfield. 'The Sutton club felt some misgivings as to the result', it was reported, 'as they had to contest against all the great cricketing talent of the neighbourhood, the Lichfield gentleman having invited several members of the Burton club to join in the game.' [93] Yet Sutton, in what was regarded as their best result since their formation, triumphed. The following summer the club comfortably defeated Oscott College. [94] That autumn members of the club gathered at the Three Tuns and 'morning's light was well nigh drawing ere the assembly concluded their annual dinner.' [95] The cricket club was the interest of a relatively small group of middle class men; the agricultural labourers who lived in Sutton probably did not even know of its existence.

Until the establishment of the Musical Institute in 1843 there was a complete absence of intellectual and cultural activity in the town. There was no newspaper, no news room, no debating society, no mechanics institute and the newly-established library was restricted to those able to pay a subscription. The Musical Institute was funded by subscriptions and there was also a ball in its aid at the town hall in February 1844 (the winter was the season for balls). The Institute sought to put on public performances each month at the town hall. The musicians who performed at the concerts – and there were usually about fifteen of them - were in the early stages of learning to play their instruments and it was noted in May 1845, after a performance featuring Boieldieu's 'Overture to the Caliph of Baghdad' and other

---

[92] Ibid., 7 August 1847.
[93] Ibid., 22 September 1849.
[94] See *Aris' Birmingham Gazette,* 18 June 1849.
[95] *Birmingham Journal,* 3 November 1849.

popular pieces, that 'the audience was highly gratified with the music and the marked improvement to the playing.' [96] At this concert the warden J.P. Oates played several solos on his tromba cornuta; he had made an improvement to this brass instrument and in January 1846 taken out a patent. [97] Even with the opportunity to hear Oates play his improved trumpet, the Musical Institute was soon dissolved.

There were many inns in Sutton. The Horse and Jockey could offer itself as a welcome stopping place for those travelling into the town from Birmingham. In 1800 it was already in existence and by 1824 could boast large front and back parlours, a kitchen, a brew house, piggeries and 'a capital kitchen garden' - and, with five bedrooms and stabling for 25 horses, could offer accommodation for the weary traveller. [98] Like other Sutton inns, the Horse and Jockey was regularly used for auctions of livestock and household furniture. The Cup also catered for travellers from Birmingham, with the landlord George Bunn in the 1840s informing 'manufacturers and others that he provides a good family dinner at one o'clock.' [99] The Old Sun could be found in Coleshill Street; in 1825 it was referred to as Robert Betts' house and in 1826 as Alice Aldridge's. [100] The Swan benefitted from travellers coming into the town from Lichfield. When Charles Spencer died in December 1828, he had been landlord for over twenty years; his niece Francis Roe took over but died in July 1833. [101] With the exception of Sundays, there were no restrictions on the opening hours of these inns, and they were frequented almost exclusively by men. The beer was brewed on the premises and was relatively weak. Nevertheless drunkenness often brought men before the Sutton magistrates.

---

[96] *Aris' Birmingham Gazette,* 26 May 1845.
[97] The tromba cornuta was not widely taken up. See ibid., 21 January 1841 for an assertion by Oates that he had invented this instrument.
[98] Ibid., 6 September 1824.
[99] *Birmingham Journal,* 26 February 1848.
[100] *Aris' Birmingham Gazette,* 25 January 1825, 15 May 1826.
[101] Ibid., 8 December 1828, 29 July 1833.

The Three Tuns was the largest and most comfortable inn in Sutton. It contained five parlours, two kitchens, a brew house and a club house often used for private dinners. With fifteen bedrooms and stabling for 26 horses, it also served as a hotel. It was catering for people travelling by coach who would break for the night at Sutton. When an important figure arrived in Sutton such as the commissioner for enclosure, the Three Tuns was where he would conduct business or spend the night. With the mail coaches stopping at the Three Tuns, the place also served as a post office. The fine houses of Sutton were usually sold by auction and it was invariably at this inn that the auctions were conducted. The Three Tuns was very much a resort of the middle class male – only at this Sutton inn could a visitor have left behind a quantity of bank notes in February 1832. For a considerable period of time the landlord of the Three Tuns was Harry Smith, aged 56 and married in 1841. In Sutton in the second quarter of the nineteenth century Smith was as well-known as any man.

A View of Sutton Coldfield by H.H. Horton

Rowton Well, Sutton Park

About the Author

Stephen Roberts holds honorary positions as Associate Professor and as a Fellow at, respectively, the Australian National University and the University of Birmingham. He is also a Fellow of the Royal Historical Society. He is the author or editor of books about both Chartism and Victorian Birmingham.

Selections from the Birmingham Biographies Series:

Sir Benjamin Stone 1838-1914: Photographer, Traveller and Politician (2014), £5.02

Sir Richard Tangye 1833-1906: A Cornish Entrepreneur in Victorian Birmingham (2015), £4.99

Joseph Chamberlain's Highbury: A Very Public Private House (2015), £3.99

Joseph Gillott and Four Other Birmingham Manufacturers (2016), £6.99

Birmingham 1889: One Year in a Victorian City (2017), £4.99

Recollections of Victorian Birmingham (2018), £4.99

Webster & Horsfall & the Atlantic Cable (2020), £4.50

George Dawson & the Church of the Saviour (2020), £3.99

These books can be ordered from Amazon and other booksellers.

Printed in Great Britain
by Amazon